such creatures

Also by Judith Thompson:

such creatures
Judith Thompson

Playwrights Canada Press
Toronto

PLAYWRIGHTS CANADA PRESS
The Canadian Drama Publisher
215 Spadina Ave., Suite 230, Toronto, ON Canada M5T 2C7
phone 416.703.0013   fax 416.408.3402
orders@playwrightscanada.com • www.playwrightscanada.com

For professional or amateur production rights, please contact
Great North Artists Management, 350 Dupont Street, Toronto, ON M5R 1V9
416.925.2051

Playwrights Canada Press acknowledges the financial support of the Government
of Canada through the Canada Book Fund and the Canada Council for the Arts,
and of the Province of Ontario through the Ontario Arts Council and the Ontario
Media Development Corporation for our publishing activities.

Canada Council
for the Arts

Conseil des Arts
du Canada

ONTARIO ARTS COUNCIL
CONSEIL DES ARTS DE L'ONTARIO

Canada

 Ontario
Ontario Media Development
Corporation

Front cover photo © Farmer Stephanie
Back cover photo © iStockphoto.com/Robert Kohlhuber
Type and cover design by Blake Sproule

LIBRARY AND ARCHIVES CANADA CATALOGUING IN PUBLICATION
Thompson, Judith, 1954-
Such creatures / Judith Thompson.

A play.
ISBN 978-0-88754-922-9

I. Title.

PS8589.H4883S83 2010   C842'.54   C2010-904909-8

First edition: September 2010
Printed and bound in Canada by Gauvin Press, Gatineau

I would like to dedicate this play to Tracy Wright, an actress of such powerful and unique spirit, a person of courage, an inspiration to me.

Such Creatures was first produced at Theatre Passe Muraille, Toronto, on January 20, 2010, with the following cast and crew:

Maria Vacratsis   Sorele
Michaela Washburn   Blandy

Directed by Brian Quirt
Production design by Beth Kates
Sound design by Justin Haynes
Stage management by Fiona Jones

Characters

Blandy
Sorele

scene one

A rundown inner-city park. High-rises loom. There is a slide, a jungle gym. These structures should be constructed so that they can be transformed into elements that might be found in a concentration camp—a bunk, an old ladder, a barbed-wire fence. The sky is dashed with dark and light blues, sunset colours, pitch-black night, and then dawn.

BLANDY   I'm peeing myself laughin' in the hall, okay? With my girls? We're like: "Yo, what up, mami?" "Nothin' much, what up wich you, girl?"

We are at Crystal's locker, decorating it crazy for her fourteenth birthday, even though I heard she was talkin' shit about me; I said to her: "I don't talk shit about you, why you talkin' shit about me?" and she didn't say nothing. I was gonna show her I don't talk shit by doin' up her locker with condoms and cigarettes and that and Perez, he walks up and I am like "OH MY GOD!" because decorating lockers is automatic suspension, eh, so I'm like passing out, and he's like: "Blandy, I wanna talk to you." I go: "What, I'm not doing nothing, asshole, are you serious? What, do you think I have a weapon? Do I look like I would carry a weapon?" and Chernelle goes: "Dry!" She's so funny, man, and he goes: "No, I'm not pissed off at you, even though you got zero on your 'all about me' skit, because you didn't prepare nothing." Well, so what I didn't prepare!? My Aunt Connie, who is really my foster mother, had took me to Casino Niagara for two days. He says: "Blandy, I want you to be the star in the play for class." I'm like: "What play? A play? That's so gay." He's like: "Don't say that, I tole you that was offensive to gay people." I go: "It's just an expression, man, it don't have nothing to do with gay people, my uncle is gay, I even hang out with him sometimes," and he goes: "Okay, okay, just don't use it to mean something cheesy." I'm like: "Okay!" Then he says: "Anyways, the play is *Hamlet*." I'm like: "What, you gotta be kidding me! I never been in a play since grade one." He's like: "You're in it." I'm like: "Okay, okay. But I don't want to look bad. Who's doin' the costumes?" He's like: "Cooper." I'm like: "COOPER? The pool teacher?" We all hate that guy, we hate getting into our bathing suits for pool because he is lookin' at our butts, right; you should see him, his eyes when he is lookin' at us? Reminds me of the look on a dog's eyes when he is eating his own vomit. So all the girls, every single one of us, have their period every time it's pool, there is like one nerdy girl in the pool who don't know about him yet 'cause she came from like Russia, yesterday. We don't want him lookin' at our butts, not because they are big, though, don't be thinkin' that, man, nobody I know worries about havin' a big butt I mean yeah, we worry about it, but you gotta be really fat to be called fat in my school. And nobody wants to be blond. In fact, if you are blond? You dye your hair brown.

So I'm like: "I'm not doin' it if Cooper is doin' the costumes," so Perez is like: "So you do your own costume," and I'm like: "YES." 'Cause I don't care what part I am playin', I am wearing my sweatpants and my hoodie and really sick shoes. All my shoes are new and all my shoes are expensive. I got fifteen pairs of shoes; if I hadda get shoes at Payless? I would kill myself. So I'm like: "What part?" He's like: "Hamlet. There's gonna be three Hamlets and two of them are girls." So I go: "Everyone's gonna be girls, you're not gonna get any boys to do the play, sir, because if you say 'play' the boys will say 'No friggin' way, a play? That's so friggin' gay!'" He goes: "I said don't say that again," I'm like: "I JUST DID!" Anyways, I go: "If you are a boy you are a baller or a skater and nothin' in between." And Perez, he's like: "I got the boys already. They have to do it, it's for class." And he gives me the script. I'm like: "You don't expect me to actually read this thing, do you?" And he goes: "I'll show you the movie but you gotta try readin' it." So I take it home and I do try to read it but I can't understand nothing. I throw it against the wall. Next day I'm like: "I'm not doin' it, I have my period." He goes: "Okay, okay, forget the script. Here is what you gotta say," and he has it all down! He says: "BLANDY, listen, and spit out your gum. Since you are Hamlet number three your first lines is 'Mother? Mother? Now, Mother, what's the matter?' You ever said that? Huh? Huh? Huh?" And he is so in my face! I'm like: "Okay, okay, yah, only every friggin' day with my mother," because my mother, Theresa? She was always freakin', and so I did, I said that to her all the time. And you know when Hamlet says "Sit you down," and she is afraid of him, so she goes: "Oh oh wilt thou kill me?" Well it's funny, that reminded me of the time I was really pissed off at my mother for getting with this shithead, right? Joseph the frickin' maniac. And just because I'm yellin' and callin' her a stupid woman and just because I pulled a knife on her, she calls the cops on me! Well, hey, I pulled the knife on her because after I called her a stupid woman she was callin' me a slut, and I was eleven! You shouldn't call your eleven-year-old daughter a slut. I told her, I said I am telling all my friends you called me that. So she says to the cops: "My daughter is trying to kill me! Boo hoo." Lyin' bitch, the cops just laughed. Then they took me away in HANDCUFFS—I am SERIOUS—and the last time I seen her? They were takin' her away in handcuffs.

So anyways, with the play? I am startin' to get it good, you know? Get it down, like a real actress, like the lines, the actions; oh I LOVE the actions, like when I get to kill that little BIGmouth Polonius, through the curtain? Because he is listening in to the fight between me and my mami? It's like I'm killin' someone in my life who I'm not sayin' who it is, someone I have killed in my heart many times, and and in the play? I go: "Thou finds to be too busy is some danger." And I'm like: "Oh my God, it's like I'm talkin' to myself because I like to talk, eh, I am BUSY BLANDY, that's what my grandmother always called me when she lived with us, eh, before she died? And I am always getting myself into trouble for telling people's secrets!

It's like I can't help it, it just falls outta my mouth like bad teeth, so it's like in that moment of killing Polonius, I am Hamlet, AND the guy he's killing, at the same time! I did kind of like that Polonius in a way, though, when he said "Neither a borrower nor a lender be because you lose your friends and the loan," because that happened to me. When I loanded Crystal my Juicy top and she still hasn't given it back. And then, oh my God, in that same "Mother Mother" scene? When I see the ghost of my father, Hamlet Senior? And like I see him and my mother, Gertrude, she don't see him, she says: "Who the frick are ya talkin' to, Hamlet?" and that is like just like in my life, when when—well—I don't really like to talk about it because I only see my stupid-ass dad when I'm feeling sick to my stomach, and my mother, she never sees him, and me? It's only ever outta the corner of my eye even, but I can tell, right, there's something he wants and he wants it so bad and it makes me just loony, I just want him outta my sight, I'm like: "Dad, go back to burning hell where ya CAME from, I don't LIKE you, I NEVER liked you; but the one I like? Is when it rains really hard? And I can't sleep and suddenly there is this flower smell in the room? And I look up and there's my grandmother, my dad's mom, Rosa Rubina, just sittin' on my bed, her cheeks all pinky. And she looks at me and she says, she whispers: "Bernadette; te amo." She calls me that, 'cause that's my name, eh, my holy name. Bernadette. After SAINT Bernadette!

So I get Hamlet, right, I get the part of him that sees GHOSTS.

And oh, oh, oh! In another part of the play? When everything is goin' real bad for him? "From this time forth my thoughts be bloody or be nothing worth." I have said that very same thing after Rochelle and them said they were gonna kill me because they thought I liked her boyfriend Shamal who goes to Oakwood.

They said they were gonna get Tania's dad's gun?

I never never said I liked him, I wouldn't say that! What happened was we was at the Dufferin Mall? In the food court? And he asked me if I would do something nasty and I said: "Do I LOOK like I'm gonna be doin' that for you, asshole?" and I sucked my teeth like my girl-friend Chernelle taught me and then I walked away. But that night I told Laurena? The one who got her eyebrows burned off? And she told Rochelle and them, so they were gonna kill me; they have killed people before, that's what my cousin said, so I said to myself, "My thoughts be bloody or be nothing worth." Just like Hamlet. And when Rochelle went to slap me I slapped her first. Left a hand mark on her face for three days.

And this lady? Maureen? She is a professional sword fighter, man, and they brought her in to teach us the fencing? I rocked at that, man, I shimmy shined, and if that tip hadn't been poisoned by Claudius and Laertes? I woulda beat him, man, I was all over it, right, with the swords makin' beautiful sounds in the air and the moves and the cape and then how he kills the bad King Claudius with the sword? Like, "TAKE THIS YOU

FRICKER, GO TO THY DEATH, GO, GO, GO!" and then he stuffs the poison pearl down his mouth? That is intensely cool, that pearl stuffing, and I so liked doing that? I could do that every night on a stage till I graduate, man.

Like I said, I GET Hamlet—but they still think I'm stupid, oh they won't SAY stupid, you know what they say? They say "LD" and then they put me in that garbage dump they call learning centre.

Basically, school is so boring I don't learn it, right? I keep fallin' asleep. So I am in with people who can't speak no English yet or who are dumb like me and I STILL don't learn nothing because now it's not only boring but it's crazy with noise and fighting and shit, so what I do? Is I think about what I DO know… Especially this one part: I got this one part perfect. So, backstory first: My moms and me—when she wasn't mental?—used to go to this so-called psychic down the street? You know, Maria? With the pink neon sign in the window? My moms and I would go to like find out what was gonna happen like with my mom's boyfriend, or her job searching, or if her dad was gonna send her money or not and what we should do, like in our lives, and this Maria, she was a piece of work, man, she was getting all this money from my mom, like every welfare cheque, and my mom was getting afraid of her, partly because she knew so much about my mom, right? And this bitch was threatening her. So I went in and I said this from the play, I said:

"Listen, you phony bitch, this whole thing is the shit. All you do is talk shit. We are not payin' you another

cent and we are not listening to your shit. We defy augury. There is special providence in the fall of a sparrow.
IF IT BE NOW, 'TIS NOT TO COME. IF IT BE NOT TO COME,
it will be now. If it be not now, yet it will come. The
readiness is all; we defy augury! Her face? Was white as
a sheet, and she never asked for money again.

I used to stay up nights sayin' that one out loud because
I really get it, right? I get that one more than any of the
other lines. "The readiness is all."

So the end, right? The end was spooky, man. Every
time we practised it I felt so spooky, because you gotta
understand, my guy, Hamlet, me, he is like—I am like
keelin' over, on the stage, with all these other people
around me dead or dying, and me, I am dying but talking, talking, like this guy I seen at that strip mall last
year? After the car came up and just shot him like eight
times and I am in the hair salon with my mother and
I come out and he is lyin' there bleeding and talking
and talking, and that is Hamlet, me, making up with
his girlfriend's brother, forgiving each other, and then,
he is taking his last breath? And he is thinking, like
thinking of the rest of time, without him talking, and
and he says to his friend Horatio, "Tell my story, man."
And that is totally me, all the time, imagining, like, the
world without me talking. Without Blandy talking shit,
and I almost can't but when I do? It is scary, man, a
scary place. So quiet a world without Blandy talking:
the rest... is... silence.

scene two

SORELE speaks from darkness to the audience.

SORELE   When we first arrived here? I thought that everyone here was blind. You know the way a blind person's eyes are? ALL the people here looked like that: I thought this must be a prison for the blind, I thought when they realize that we are not blind they will surely free us! I was thirteen. I still believed in God...

Within a day or so, everyone I came with,
they looked blind also.

Not Them, though. Oh no. Their eyes were bright, with the brightness of... an eclipse.

And brighter with every atrocity.

I don't know if I looked like I was blind or not;
I know that I saw everything.
And I have been able to forget nothing.

To be back here, forty years later... is...

She takes time, looks around, feels it.

I don't think there is a word for it.

Imagine me before all... this. *(She gestures around her.)* A rosy-faced thirteen-year-old brat, with much mischief in my eyes, always a wicked smile on the edge of my mouth, I never walked, I skipped or RAN! I had just played Miranda in *The Tempest* at my school, I was on top of the world.

But then? After two years here?

In January 1945, "liberation day" right here in this very room, what I am? Sixty-three pounds, skin yellow, almost GREEN—stretched over my bones. I have no hair, well, a few wisps, my teeth have fallen out, my nails have fallen out... blue lips, fast raspy breathing, eyes rolling back.

I do not look human. I do not look alive.

If you gave me food, it would kill me. If I don't get medical care I will die within... a day. If you saw me? You would think, "It's better if she dies."

So, now, forty years ago today, this very day, that is me, and I am hiding in a pile of naked bodies. I know, it's a

terrible thing to tell you, but it's true. All of us, emaci-
ated of course. Feet, feet everywhere around me, open
mouths staring, eyes, hip bones, ribs... hands. I am
hiding, here, in the bodies of my friends. Well, some
are my friends, some I didn't like... many, I didn't
know.

And I am deciding, with the one part of my brain that is
still clear, whether to melt into these bodies, and take
my last breath with them...

OR...

To raise my hand when the Russians come in.
To raise my hand and choose... a life...
I have only minutes to decide...

So, imagine me, in all these naked bodies with dead staring eyes, my eyes are the only eyes seeing, the only eyes
LOOKING out from the pile, but if you were to see me,
you wouldn't be sure if I was dead or alive because, although my eyes are moving, my body is still, as still as
the others—I do not have the strength to speak, even
a whisper, but I, I could maybe, just MAYBE, raise my
hand, I could do that, if I wanted them to... notice me.
But! I am not sure I do: I have heard that the Russian
soldiers are raping women, not just German women,
even us! so if I raise my hand THAT could happen, which
would instantly kill me anyway; a dismal refugee camp
could happen; lynching could happen, YES, it happened
to MANY; OR, OR, POSSIBLY, BEST scenario, I could say
I was SWEDISH, and be sent to Sweden for vanilla ice
cream, CREAMY vanilla ice cream, which would be going to heaven, but then, AFTER eating ice cream, then I

would have to live on this earth, that's what I was fearing. Another seventy or eighty years. To an old, old lady, who will wake screaming with night terror, after dreaming of my sister, hanging from a rope.

That's what I am fearing while I lie in the pile of bodies and listening to the Russian soldiers outside, and the cheers of the survivors, and the shooting, the beautiful shooting.

Please. Don't feel sad for the girl that I was, lying here. There is something calm about being near death, you know the feeling of lying in a snowbank and looking at the stars, when it's not too cold, and the snowflakes are falling on your face, and you could just lie there forever?

And I had my certainty, the sweet certainty that this would never happen again; the world would be warned and never will the innocent be brutalized again.

NEVER NEVER NEVER NEVER NEVER.

That is what I believed.

"Cans't thou remember a time before we came unto this cell?"

We girls were on our way to work in the factory, a voice from Block 25 shouted this out. I tried to ignore it but then he said it again. His EYES were staring at me, wildly, his mouth open, foaming—

"Cans't thou remember a time before we came unto this cell?"

I wondered, who was this man, was he an actor, or a
famous director, or MAYBE, a teacher from my school in
Warsaw who saw me in my most glorious moment as
Miranda in *The Tempest*? How did he know these words?
I was just about to ask him this when one of the Greek
girls, she sobbed out to me: "SORELE! They're going to
kill us today, please take this note to my cousin Amalia,
please!" I knew I had to turn away immediately from
her or the kapo would throw me in with her and I too
would be smoke and ash by lunchtime, but even still I
couldn't help it, I looked at the man right in the eye
and said:

"'Tis far off, and rather like a dream than an assurance."

What Miranda answers to her father when he asks her
that question in the play! I still remembered! And I
must say I said it REALLY well, even better than I had
said it on the stage because, because I finally GOT it, the
meaning of the LINE, it was TRUE: for me and for most
of us here our lives before were vanished, not real at
all, exactly like a far-off dream. Well that man was now
transformed. He no longer knew that he was waiting
to be murdered: only the island was real. As I walked
away from him, I could hear him say, "Approach, my
Ariel, come brave spirit!" with such joy in his voice!

For him, this—was a Mercy.

But for me? This world of hell was still real. It felt as if
this was the only world I had ever known, I seriously
doubted all my life before this: every precious mem-
ory was fading, even the faces, of everyone I loved,
disappearing—I felt myself disappearing.

So I decided then and there. That this disappearing of my world would STOP. Now. I would NEVER let THEM persuade me that their world was THE world. This WAS NOT MY world, not my LIFE, and the way for that? Was just like the mysterious man. I had to conjure my world in my mind, my island, the real true world, and I would do that by Remembering, every stupid, precious detail of my life, from brushing my teeth, to singing in the choir with my sisters, to spitting out a piece of chicken I didn't like, to turning around and seeing a boy I liked looking at me, to the beautiful sight of green grass under melting snow, to my mouth full of vanilla ice cream with caramel sauce, a leaf falling from a tree and landing on my shoulder, a cat running across the street, every little thing, you see? THIS was my REVO-LUTION, to keep my LIFE alive in my MIND. Listen, this takes CRAZY concentration; this is almost impossible to do when you are starving and trembling and sick with open boils and sores all over but I did it! My FIRST act of revolution: to remember.

scene three

BLANDY

I am so ready.
My fingers? Feel like a firecracker.
My feet? Like pistols.
My eyes? Like, like specks of SHINING ice, don't you think?

Beat.

Bring it on, Rochelle. I will tear you ALL to pieces.

I am so ready.

Listen,
I wasn't gonna sit and wait for Rochelle to AMBUSH me when I was alone, right? I'm not gonna be some frickin' rabbit sittin' in a cage waiting to be cooked. I

said, I go to Rochelle, you want to fight me? Because you think I did something I did not do? When the clock strikes twelve. You bring your girls, I bring mine. Bring body and soul and nothing else, no knives, no gats, no baseball bats.

Don't get me wrong, I hate violence for no reason. But if there is a reason? Like in a WAR, when it's kill or be killed?

We do what we have to do. And it is a war out here, trust me.

But...

If I had it my way? If this was the ideal world? I would use only words—

Like yesterday in the Burger King, I seen the girl who started this mess, YO, the one got me in the shit with Rochelle, and I KNOW this, people TOLE me this, and she is there with her onion rings, so I go up to her and I remove the onion rings and I say: "Okay I'm not gonna punch you out. I'm not gonna call you no dirty names. I just wanna ask you, politely:

"R... U... the bitch... that TOLE the bitch that I'm A SNITCH? Did you tell Rochelle I said her boyfriend's brother was talking to the cops? And so she thinks it's because of me he got shot last weekend? I wouldn't never, never, you lying bitch, because everyone knows snitching is megadeath. MEGADEATH. Why did you lie?"

And she starts laughing. I'm like: "YOU may laugh, but you gonna find out tomorrow the monster shit you stirred up, and that shit's gonna be all on you, so I am just telling you if things go as bad as they COULD go? If any of my girls get hurt? You don't wanna HEAR the Song of Bernadette."

That girl is lucky, man.

'Cause I shown her mercy.

If you woulda known me before? I didn't have no mercy. Since I was like five years old. Even then, if a Barbie pissed me off, I would tear off her head. If the teddy bear wouldn't talk? I would drown him in the sink. I didn't take shit from nobody, even toys. I was brought up from my old man that you make people pay, if you don't make people pay, they gonna do it again and YOU LOSE and you DESERVE to lose because you are a loser.

SORELE   I fought like a wildcat to survive this place;

And again I am facing my death.

Twice I have wrestled with cancer, and I had seven beautiful years without it, but now it's back. For the third time. I can feel it, spreading through my brain like mushrooms through the garden. But I do not know if I can face this again, so I wanted to come back to my first hell.

The one I made it through.

I am here to find that wildcat.

BLANDY   I was TOTALLY my father's daughter—I beat up people ALL THE TIME. No really, I was some kinda baby delinquent. I got kicked outta nine elementary schools; I would chase after grade sixes when I was in grade three, with baseball bats, swearin' at them, DIRTY mouth, dirty hands, I'd steal their money, throw their shoes on the roof, pull their hair right outta their head; made a little grade two ask the teacher if she had washed her bush that day—THAT one was funny, man—I hadda have a social worker with me full-time, even they were scared shitless of me; I could do ANYTHING, you know?

And nothing would happen to me.

Looks at her cell.

My girls are just as pumped as me. They are ON side: LEO MEENA AMITA SHANDELLE KAYLA CRYSTAL CHERNELLE HAYLEY MARIA LAURA LINDA and LACY-MARIE.

All TWELVE of them, they are putting on their kickin' shoes. They are ON the MOVE!

She dances, sort of sings.

Oh yeah, oh yeah, my girls are on the move,
On the move, on the move!

SORELE   I know it's hard to believe, but we... played!
At night, in the block? We would play a game called "delicious."

One by one we would name the food we were thinking about.

Sugary almonds, licking off the sugar.
Hot, moist bagels, covered in poppy seeds, six of them
on my papa's arm—that's what my sister would say.
Banana-shaped chocolates with banana cream oozing
out.
Coconutty macaroons, chocolate eclairs—that was
Regina.
Cakes for Purim slathered in pink whipped cream—
for Ala—and Rosa, she always wanted roast chicken
and potatoes, warm and filling and...

I have no appetite at all now.
It's all I could think of then.

BLANDY   I try to forget about you when there's people around,
but sometimes? I have been caught, eh, talking to you,
like this, because I can't help it, 'cause I feel you watchin' me, watchin' my life, and people in my school are
starting to say that I'm on crack. I told them that is a
lie, I SEEN people on crack, I seen my DAD on crack
and that is the lowest of the low, man, when you are
on crack? You are on your knees. You are on your knees
and you are suckin' the devil's...

SORELE   Yes, we played delicious every night, and also as we
stood for hours and hours in *Appel*—always shifting
places so no girls would have to be at the front or the
back too long in the freezing wind—as we watched
those who were caught with pieces of string or a
speck of soap in their *beutel* being attacked by the
dogs, as we watched those who collapsed being
taken away by the kapos, of course never to return,
as we worked like manic zombies in the gunpowder
factory.

It was terrible about the dogs, because I used to love dogs more than ANYONE. I always thought I had a special connection with dogs. We had an adorable mutt, Sammy. But now? After seeing them tear apart my friends? I hate them. I can't even be in the same room with one now.

I learned to hate very well here.

One day? A very handsome, well, handsome for HERE, this man, maybe nineteen? Who had always flirted with me, you know, with the eyes? With the sweetest smile he offered me a bracelet... It was shining in the sun, real gold, with what looked like... emeralds, and so of course I was dazzled. I let him put it on my tiny wrist, and I giggled, but then, it hit me like a punch in the stomach... who the hell it was I had been flirting with.

I SPAT in his FACE: "You think I don't know that you pulled this from the wrist of a body you burned? The body of a young girl who, who you yelled at to undress, who you lied to about showers, who you kicked through the door and locked inside a gas chamber, whose screams you tried to drown out with motorcycle engines?

"Whose screams you listened to for twenty minutes? Whose body you shoved into the fires? Whose ashes you... How dare you insult me like this. You think I would decorate my wrist with the blood of a sister? Never!"

I was so proud of myself, so PROUD I said again:

"NEVER," and I looked at him with ALL MY hatred and you know what he said?

"Yes, yes, you are right, we are the hands of Satan but we are the most wretched…"

I said "Shut up with all that, shut up and just tell me why. Why would you choose this over death?"

"REVENGE," he whispered.

"For the girl who wore this bracelet, for the little red-haired French boy who waved goodbye to the moon before he was gassed, for the grandmother who forgave me and for the other who spat in my face."

I said: "I get it. I get it."

"But I still hate you even more than I hate them. What I wish for you? Is to be torn to pieces every day for eternity by a pack of starving dogs."

I was fourteen years old, I was no longer a girl.

BLANDY

I go to Rochelle, I go: "No gats, no knives, no baseball bats, let's show the boys how its done. Because I never said nothing to NOBODY and I don't like you telling people I did, I got a reputation to defend; we fight with just our own sweet selves," and Rochelle? She's like: "Fine."

I gotta give her that, she's got guts. And she's got honour, too, she gave me her word. So I believe. I said: "Don't tell nobody, or we get the boys out, and a girl fight is not a dogfight, or a cockfight, or a fricking striptease."

Once…

I beat up this girl, Davida? In the washroom so bad I broke her nose and she passed out. I know. But… she was callin' me a crackwhore during a math test. And so not only was she trashin' me but she made me fail math again.

AGAIN.

And summer school sucks ASS, man, and applied math? Is a frickin' zoo. Yesterday? They locked the teacher out of the class, I am not kidding, they are all on their cellphones, or lookin' at porn on their phones, whatever, talking trash, I do NOT belong in special ED, dude, that is a BIG mistake. It's just because the teachers don't like me, 'cause I won't take their SHIT.

The teachers? think I am stupid, just because I fail. Jus' because you FAIL does not mean you are stupid. There is lots of reasons kids fail, you know what I'm sayin'? Just because I can't pass nothing in school except for Perez? Don't mean I am not goin' on to higher education. There are other ways to GO; Ms. Griffin the guidance, she tole me, it's called like "goin' later," something like that, after you worked and got some age on you.

And she tole me I could still get a prize.
If I get a prize at graduation? I would be like—
—I would say like…
Yeah, right.

Like, what prize could I get?
Like maybe the ugliest face?
Maybe, the ugliest body?

Maybe the ugliest personality?
Maybe the one everybody in the school hates?

I'm only kidding. Actually I am very self-confident in myself. Other girls are always like: "Oh I'm so ugly, I'm so fat, the guys don't think I'm pretty," I'm like: "Shut up. You are so boring." Whiny girls are so boring, man.

Most girls? Are pathetic.

SORELE   That was when my fear turned to fire. And fire gave me courage…
The courage I hope I will find here.
Playing delicious, it just wasn't enough.

One spring day all the girls in my block, about a hundred of us, were ordered to whip and beat a Slovakian girl named Ella who had dropped her soup bowl because her hands were trembling: he yelled and he screamed and he threatened DEATH, immediate death for all of us, and you know what? There was a long, long silence, he yelled again, but what happened is that not one of us moved. We were still, like children playing statue we did not move a finger, we did not shift or blink or even breathe.

We fully expected to be tortured if not killed, but at that point we didn't care, we had nothing to lose, we were not going to kill our friend, you can do anything you want to me but you will NOT make me less than human… and so they told us we were all going to die for this. That day. They said "Wait here, cockroaches, by night you will be ash."

We waited and waited and we prayed and held on to each other, hour after hour, and then dawn and then… unbelievably, they came, as if nothing had happened, and we were marched to work again.

You know, evil of course is much more powerful than good. But sometimes? Good gets a good kick in!

BLANDY —Hey, you ever imagined what purgatory is?

I KNOW what it is. I so know, I'm'onna write the Pope and tell him! I figured it out!

It's school.

Sometimes it's so so so so boring with a capital B I think I'm gonna like combust into flames like a barbeque, you know what I'm saying? I heard that could happen to a human, in Europe or Russia or the subway, whatever, it happened. Of BOREDOM.

But you know what? I would rather go to hell than spend the rest of eternity in school, and that's a good thing 'cause that's where I'm goin', and you know why?

Because TONIGHT? I'm not gonna show no mercy.

I can NOT show mercy tonight because yo, if I back down? They are gonna finish me right here, and if they don't finish me tonight? They will take their sweet time but they will finish me. Look, you can't run away 'cause there's nowhere to run to if they want to find you, they will find you. Hey, you don't know what it's like out here, you think it's only guys, the news always tells about the guys getting shot, et cetera, but we girls, we got it bad. It is BAD out here.

When I was growing up? I was small, eh, small for my age? And I couldn't walk to school without getting beat up. Every single day, they would wait for me, till one day, I went CRAZY, yelling and punchin' and scratchin' like a maniac. From then on, they didn't touch me, and I hadda stay maniac.

I gotta show 'em, that I am the stronger.

I am the scarier, I am the ROTTWEILER.

You gotta OUT EVIL the evil, that is the only way. You can't fight EVIL with Peacefulness, right? You understand that?

You can try all that social worker shit you want, let's talk it out, it's a misunderstanding, stop the cycle of violence, we all know all that shit backwards and forwards. When you are in the situation I am in? It don't mean shit.

If I want to survive, I gotta show 'em what's what.
Maybe after tonight? I'll go away somewhere.
Use the money from my gramma and just take off, to Texas, see my half brothers.

A church bell sounds eleven times.

Bring it ON.

27

SORELE   So that act of NOT moving, that... gave me the... courage... to... MOVE! Listen, you know those stories of the circus, has a crash on the highway? And even though the door to the lion cage is open it takes the lion three hours to... realize? Well that was me, on that day... at the gunpowder factory, when after twelve or thirteen hours of the usual hideous and filthy and backbreaking work, I raised my head, I raised my head and I REALIZED: there is no yelling, nobody was yelling at us or swatting us across the face, no kapo, no SS, nobody was being beaten up to a bloody pulp for sniffling. Hey, there was NOBODY watching us. NOBODY. And clearly, nobody was coming. But we were all still heads down, working as fast as we could, terrified, but me, I looked around. I was like the lion, the circus lion seeing, understanding, that the cage is open. It is WIDE open. So for the first time, in seventeen months, I moved... away from the table. I INCHED. Away... like... *(She demonstrates.)* Can you imagine what that felt like? I walked—at first one foot, then two feet, and then? Across the whole factory room. I felt FREEDOM, inside I was shouting like Caliban: Freedom High Day, Freedom HIGH day. Freedom.

Suddenly my mind was sharp, my eyes saw everything, I saw this and I saw that, and how things work and who exactly did what.

And that is when I knew.

I knew exactly what we had to do.

BLANDY   "I could be bounded by a nutshell and count myself king of infinite space were it not for my bad dreams..."

The worst dream I had? Is that my gramma died. Right beside me, see, we used to share a bed? Because there wasn't enough beds, eh. At first I slept under the bed 'cause I didn't want to catch her oldness, but after a while the floor was too hard. We would laugh, and tell secrets, and she used to sing to me in her language and I felt like being with her was the safest place in the world, even though she snored I didn't even mind. She was in a way my real mother so I used to have these nightmares that she was dead and then one morning I woke up and I had the nightmare awake: she... looked like a doll, her face was not her face. Her eyes were open but not SEEING, she wasn't breathin' so I did the mouth-to-mouth I'd seen on TV and the punchin' her chest but that was it, man. She was gone. She was dead. I phoned 911 and the sirens came and...

Lookin' at them take her away? I felt a hole the size of a dinner plate in my chest. I still have it there. But it's like the plate broke inside.

Don't tell nobody but we paid a guy at the funeral place off and we got her body back and we buried her in the backyard because she loved her garden. She had planted tomatoes, and roses, and green ferns; that's where she wanted to be, she did NOT want to be in some stone-cold cemetery with all them people she didn't even know. I always wear this cross she gave me, and I always will. You'd have to kill me to get it off me.

SORELE   This was a gunpowder factory; we handled the gunpowder every minute of every day, that's why they put us in there, the starving, half-crazed teenaged girls,

they never imagined that we would get up to anything—so I went with my plan to the men who had
been planning some kind of revolt...

See, the *sonderkommando* had figured out that they were
going to be killed in three months and replaced so they
decided they would fight to the death. Because of the
extra food they were given, they were stronger than
the rest of us. so for months and months they had been
gathering weapons, guns from the partisans, they already had knives and axes for their atrocious work, so
when the SS came for them they were going to fight to
the death—so here I was a very sickly fourteen-year-
old girl, and I said to them: "Listen, I have a way to
help you... to blow up a crematorium; a sure way."
Only that would slow down the killing—thousands
of Hungarians were still arriving daily and being sent
straight to the gas chambers. They were very happy
with me, I was... ready...

And so, we devised a plan; I had to have help, and I had
to be very careful, so I recruited my very best friends
in the world: Rosa and Ala and Regina and my sister.

BLANDY   When I think about it, you know? My reputation for
talking? Began a long time ago, when I told about
Rochelle's baby.

I was only fourteen, man, and it's big news when someone has a baby, someone in your grade; especially when
the father is her BROTHER. I couldn't help it, I only told
Melena's brother Renaldo when I was smashed on the
rum that Patrick brought back from Jamaica, I can't
help what comes out when I'm drinkin'. When I'm

drinkin' I'm EXTRA. When people are drinking? They are more themselves and less themselves. You know what I'm sayin'?

SORELE   That night in the bunk while lying in each other's arms I said, I said to my sister, "It's time." When I explained my idea she said, "Stop, little sister, don't even talk like that. If we just do what we are told the Allies will come in the next few months and maybe we will be free, if we do THIS, we'll be for CERTAIN caught and killed." I looked into her eyes, I looked miles deep into her eyes, and I whispered, "Wilt thou go with me?" And after a long time we fell asleep in each others arms, her warm breath on my neck. I think we dreamed the same dream.

BLANDY   My foster mother Connie? Is a douche. I have to ask permission to use the bathroom. And she listens in on all my calls. And threatens to send me back to Children's Aid EVERY frickin' day.

I'm thinking... of, after this? Goin' to a group home.

Or... Covenant House. But then they kick you out when you're sixteen. so even... if I have to? Sleepin' rough. For a while. You know, movin' around.

SORELE   My sister, and Ala, and Rosa, and Regina, and me—we had... readiness, you know?

The coarse, smelly, black gunpowder that we handled every minute of every day could save thousands and thousands of lives. They thought we were all too BLIND to see what was RIGHT in front of us. But not all of us were blinded.

So. What we did? Every single day, each of us would sneak about a teaspoon of that black grainy gunpowder into our beutels... some days we couldn't, but most days we could, and if there was an inspection? We could secretly empty the gunpowder into the dirt and smoosh it around with our feet. They never suspected ANYTHING.

Robel, the one who tried to give me the gold bracelet? He and a few of the others would come to our side to pick up the bodies of girls who had been killed by a bad-tempered kapo or died from typhus, and Rosa, she would hide the gunpowder we had collected that day either in a sack by the fence or in... yes, even in the bodies, so even the dead were helping us, and then Robel would take it back to the men's camp, and then, this Russian army fellow, Borodin, who knew explosives, was able to make a hand grenade using shoe-polish tins filled with the gunpowder. SHOE POLISH and gunpowder, can you believe this? It was the shoe polish used to polish the boots of the SS.

Now, you know and I know, with every plan? Even the most perfectly worked out plan in the world?

Something will always go wrong.

BLANDY   My moms? ...She never even tole me what we ARE, you know? Like all the other kids KNOW they are Jamaican, or American, or Chinese, or Korean, or even Canadian, but me? I don't know what the frick I am. It BURNS me. My mom? She like hints around at something, she will go: "Walk into a room like you own it because you DO, Blandy, you own the room and the floor and the ground underneath it. This is YOUR LAND," she will say, but then she says to me she will never tell me 'cause she doesn't want me to live through what she lived through growin' up. I used to yell at her: "WHAT AM I, Mom, WHAT the HELL am I?"

Oh, and before she went mental she was a professional stealer and, man, when she was doin' that? We ate out all the time, Swiss Chalet, Thai, Indian, KFC, whatever we wanted. It was like we were travelling, you know? Travellin' over the world.

SORELE   There had been a RAT amongst us; someone had be-
trayed us, for a hunk of bread, or an extra day of
life... This happened all the time, informers EVERY-
WHERE, and often those you least suspect... I learned
then to never trust anybody, I'm sorry, but its true...
Five weeks before the day we had carefully planned
on we heard the Germans, rounding up the men. I
thought for sure our revolt was doomed, then someone yelled in Yiddish: "NIK-KUM-E!" They were going ahead, ready or not they had NOTHING to lose.
They all were yelling "Revenge revenge, kill the dev-
ils."They attacked the SS with axes, hammers, killing
them right there and then.

And remember Robel? You know what he did? He
grabbed the most sadistic SS, that would throw children live into the fire? And he personally fed him
into the oven. Everyone cheered. Then while the
SS were running around like chickens, we threw
the grenades and bombs we had made at the crema-
toria. Crematorium FOUR was blown up. DESTROYED.
Thousands and thousands of lives spared because
of us. FIVE not-so-silly teenaged girls. I look at my

daughters, sixteen, ninteen, and twenty-three, and...
I can't even begin to imagine...

I flam'd amazement; sometime I'd divide,
And burn in many places; on the topmast,
The yards, and boresprit, would I flame distinctly,
The fire and cracks
Of sulphurous roaring the most mighty Neptune
Seem to besiege and make his bold waves tremble,
Yea, his dread trident shake.

I cut a hole in the fence myself and six hundred men
went through.
We, the gunpowder girls, created a tempest, we blew
The evil ship to smithereens.

We Jews, we fought back.

And we are still fighting back.

Long beat.

Will we ever stop fighting back...

BLANDY   ...The other day? In the Dufferin Mall? We're in the
food court, eatin' their shitty shawarma, and I see this
guy, about forty, with a cat in his arms, comin' towards
me and I realize it's my DAD again. My DAD is a frickin'
GHOST and he is HAUNTING me, nobody else can see
him. I don't want to see him, because I don't have NO
respect for him. He was even HOMELESS the last part
of his life, I would, like, see him on the street? He'd
be like: "Hey, sweetheart, come and give your daddy
a hug." I'd pretend I didn't know him. Because as far

as I was concerned, he'd just given up, like all home-less, ya know, given up on life. But one time, around Christmas? I felt sorry for him, so I gave him my lunch money, and ya know what he told me?

That most of the homeless guys you see? Like sleepin' on the sidewalk and that? Are ghosts. They are real live ghosts, like people who have died a long time ago and gone to hell and that's why they talk so crazy some of them, and they don't like sleepin' inside, and they sleep outside when it's freezing frickin' cold, and their hands are so dirty, and their faces like stone, and their hair, like, like snakes, and they won't come in because they are in hell, right? They are bad people that went to hell, sinners, and so when they got there, they were com-manded by GOD, himself, to walk the earth to the end of time. To always be cold, always be hungry and always be angry and never be touched.

My very very very worst fear? In fact my ONLY fear? What keeps me awake sometimes at night?

Is that I become one of them.

SORELE   I wondered... if... I would feel the ghosts, the spirits of all the hundreds of thousands of human beings mur-dered here.

But they are not here.

What would they want to hang around here for?

When a girl stopped playing delicious, we knew that she had given up, and that she would not last. She was a "*musselman*," that's what we called them, those who had given up.

You've seen their pictures, they looked like… a cross between someone dying of terminal cancer and the half-crazed homeless you see on our streets…

They had given up… hope.

I'll tell you the truth: I don't have much hope left. Because I have done my research. A third metastases almost always means "goodbye." I would never tell my family that; to them, I pretend.

I have written… each of my children, three daughters and two sons, letters, to be sent to them wherever they are once a year for the next twenty years… Is that too much? Maybe after a while they won't read them, maybe after a while they shouldn't… But I have written the letters anyway, and on the front I have written "Don't open if you don't feel like it." What do you think? Is that too much?

Like you,
I believe in reasonable hope.
Not… fairy tale hope.
Although I do like fairy tales; who doesn't?

BLANDY   You don't think this is serious?
You think this is teenaged girls pullin' hair?

In my school you can get TOTALLY killed for havin' a big mouth. Or suckin' your teeth or rollin' your frickin' eyes at someone. Or lookin' at someone.

There is certain people? Don't like to be LOOKED at. I know someone who knows someone who got stabbed to death for laughin' at karaoke.

SORELE   But it was because of this fairy tale hope, I think, that so many went obediently to their deaths, quietly, waiting in the birch trees, naked, even folding their clothes, removing their watches, their eyeglasses, calming their children with lullabies—hiding their infants under the piles of coats, they hoped that someone would have mercy, they hoped that the worst could not possibly be true, they HOPED… that they would wake up from this ravaging dream, they hoped that the soldiers were human beings who would suddenly take pity on innocent children, they hoped that they might be the one who survived the bullet to the head and would crawl out from the pile of bodies—they HOPED for a MIRACLE and NO MIRACLE happened.

BLANDY   *You know* Bernadette of Lourdes? In France? In WAY olden days, like medieval times? Do you KNOW her? SHE had a miracle happen to her. Okay, she was TOTAL-LY like me, a dumb but really smart peasant girl with a welfare family, and what happened to her? She's in this grotto, pickin' berries, and suddenly she feels a… a… shimmering.

Like, Niagara Falls rushin' through her.

And then her whole body starts to shiver and the world turns this shade of unsayable colour and what she sees in front of her? Through the mist? Is a lady, the most outrageously beautiful lady she has ever seen, with brilliant light shining right out of her. It's MARY Mother

37

of GOD. She is smiling at Bernadette and the smile is so summer warm it stops her shivers, and makes flowers bloom inside her, and the lady's hands? Her hands are like little white DOVES.

The eyes, too, the lady's eyes look right at Bernadette, miles deep into her eyes, and she whispers to her the secret of the world, the secret of the whole world, and then the mist, the mist breezes away, and reveals the foot, the foot of the lady, on top, on top of a... serpent, the most worst fugliest serpent of all—is Satan—a EVIL snake with the head of Satan, eyes like shit on fire, and she's got her little soft foot on top of his head and he is DEFEATED.

I sometimes imagine that I am Bernadette with... that light on my face. With her hands on my head, she is telling me the secret of the world.

SORELE   When we first arrived, all falling out of the cattle cars, so many dead, gasping for air, the screaming, the barking, the lights in our eyes, the lunatics yelling for our jewellery.

I held onto my mother for dear life, everyone else, my father, my sisters, had vanished, into the crowd, we were thousands, but we still... hoped for the best: many of us were dressed in our finest... clothes; it was the fashion to wear colourful ribbons, on everything, in our hair, on our socks, around the waist, like pretty wrapped presents; when I arrived I was wearing a beautiful green plaid dress with a crisp green ribbon around my waist... I suppose we thought if we were well-dressed... a young German soldier looked at me, pulled at my coat and he said, "Come here, pretty girl," and he looked at my mother and said, "The girl will be safer if you are not together." "I will never leave my daughter," said my mother. He said: "You are old. If she stays with you, you will both die."

BLANDY That was my grandmother's favourite movie, *The Song Of Bernadette*? We used to watch it every Sunday.

Me and Gramma, curled up in the one chair, and when, every time Bernadette saw the lady? The LIGHT, the light that would be on her FACE was on my grandmother's face and my face together and it was the light of GOD.

SORELE My mother, her eyes became as green as an evergreen like they always did when she was crying without tears, and she took my hands and kissed my face. He said "Hurry," she ran off into the crowd with that coat of hers, that brown coat with the black fur I always teased her about. The next time I saw that coat was on one of the German Jewish girls working Kanada Commando.

We didn't like the German girls... they always thought they were better than us, and they always got the best jobs because they spoke German.

BLANDY I been thinking about it? And every person in the world has something that they are afraid of that don't seem to make no sense: you, even you all of you, got something you are afraid of that don't make any sense, like my two-year-old cousin, he's scared of seaweed. My uncle, he is this big scary-lookin' guy, he's a contractor, right? He's a scared of the dark. Has to sleep with the light on. I know a lot of people scared of cats. My gramma was scared of people with red hair, I would go: "GRAMMA they can't HELP it," and she would be shakin'! So everybody has their thing they're a scared of, every single person you know, and if you find that? If you find out that about a person? You could scare them to death.

She's on her way now, I can feel it, I can feel it in my BODY.

Like what that bad king says about Hamlet,
"Like the hectic in the blood she rages..."

Yo. I am the hectic ragin' in her blood.
She the evil weasel
wants to kill me in the mud.

Rochelle, YOU hell,
You gonna be shocked,
You gonna be ROCKED,
You know I didn't tell.

SORELE   Of course, with the help of the villagers, all of the rebels were caught, ALL OF THEM, and forced to lie on their stomachs and shot in the back of the head, almost six hundred shots we heard, except for the few they kept for interrogation. When I hear... shots... in the movies, or on television, it's as if I was there again, as if no time has passed, and I... am... overwhelmed...

I didn't go through the fence myself, because... I knew... this is what would happen... ONE of those they questioned was Robel, the one who tried to give me the bracelet? And this coward? He gave up my sister, and Ala, and Roza, and even Regina, who was just our lookout. Poor Regina.

HE DID NOT GIVE MY NAME. Why did he not give up my name?

Because he… I can't even say it…

My beloved sister and the other girls were put in a prison hell even worse hell than our prison, they were tortured for three months… we could all hear their screams. October, November, December. I didn't see my sister once in all that time, but I could feel her agony. I only wanted to be in there with her… but I didn't, I did not give myself up… I could say it was because I knew my sister wanted me to survive to tell the world, but really, it was me, it was because I wanted to live. And you know? These teenaged girls? The only names THEY gave up were those of sonderkommando already dead.

They did not give up my name.

Would I have given up theirs?

BLANDY   Watch out, Rochelle,
              Watch your back, big bell,
              'Cause when Blandy through with you,
              You gonna be in HELL.
              Been ragin' in her blood,
              Rochelle Rochelle.

SORELE   While my sister and the others were in there, I thought a lot about *The Tempest*.

I thought about this camp as the island, and the SS as Prospero, and I realized that I was not Miranda, I was not even Ariel, I was Caliban. We were all Caliban.

"Here you sty me
In this hard rock, whiles you do keep from me
The rest o' the island."

The SS used words that Prospero used:

"Lying slaves,
Whom stripes may move, not kindness!
Filth. Abhorred slave,
capable of all ill!"
They call us savage, our language
Brutish, gabble. If we speak Yiddish we are beaten.
They refer to us as a
Vile race, vile vile vile,
When I played Miranda, I hated Caliban.

BLANDY   See, I gotta scare her off me for good, right? I gotta be the FOOT stompin' down on the SERPENT; that's gotta be me and I may not like it, I don't LIKE the sight of blood, dude, or broken teeth, but at least I'm doin' something, PROVIN' something, BEING who I AM. It's better than goin' to Mickey D's and walkin' around goin' to the park, goin' to the FOOD court and the frickin' MALL, watchin' TV and doin' nothing. Fighting for your life is doin' something.

When they get here? My girls? Leopoldina, Meena and Amita and Shandelle and Kayla and Crystal and Chernelle and Hayley and Maria and Laura and Linda and Lacy-Marie? You are gonna see how kickin' they

are, man, I LOVE my girlfriends, I mean I love them and
they love me and nobody outside of us understands how
much we are FOR each other, right? I mean that is LOVE
bigger than any boyfriend; boys? Are TOYS for us, right?
And stylin'? Oh my God you think I have style? My girls?
They know how to DRESS. Exspecially Leo. She is class,
she's goin' into fashion design, she gonna have her own
line, and Amita? She could be a model RIGHT NOW, cover
of a magazine, she gotta turn a hose on the guys to keep
them away, and my girls? They KNOW how to SCRAP, too,
we are like a female fight club, we practise? All the time,
in the school parking lot, all night till dawn breaks.

And every one of them, can KICK ASS.

SORELE   And now I'm becoming Caliban again: as I get sicker,
with the treatments, losing my hair, my eyelashes, my
balance, my face will be bloated with the steroids, and
yellow, I will look like the monster.

"I prithee, let me bring thee where crabs grow;
And I with my long nails will dig thee pignuts;
Show thee a jay's nest and instruct thee how
To snare the nimble marmoset."

(I was one of those annoying actresses who knew everyone's part and has never forgotten a single line of
the play in forty-two years.)

"I'll bring thee
To clustering filberts and sometimes I'll get thee
Young scamels from the rock. Wilt thou go with me?"

Wilt thou go with me?

BLANDY

Hey, did you know I got hit by a car?
Did I not TELL you?

I am walkin' on Vaughan Road with my girls, we are talking shit, we are laughing, laughing so hard. about something Mr. Picou said, Serene peed her pants because she is pregnant so she can't hold it, right? And that made me laugh so hard I wasn't thinking I guess, so we hadda cross to go get smokes and chips and that, well I am lookin' if Monica's nose ring is infected and I step onto St. Clair and WHAAAAP, I am hit by a TAXI, I am on the windshield bouncing off.

I am on the street, blood SPRAYING from my mouth, I am thinking I lost all my teeth, that's okay, Moms has no teeth, my aunt has no teeth, you can live with no teeth.

And Crystal is there and Audrey and Chernelle and Leopoldina, they're like: "BLANDY, we're takin' you to hospital," but I'm getting up? I get up and I walk!

I am walkin' along like a bee that you hit with a book, you seen that?
And no matter what they do to me tonight?
I am gonna be that BEE. I am gonna get up and I am gonna walk away.
Me and my Leopoldina, and all my girls, arm in arm we will be walkin' away...

SORELE

I was worried, that when you, the people of the future, looked at pictures of us, even at the moving pictures that the SS always took of us, that we would look so different, different from you, our hair, our fashions, even the expressions on our faces, that you wouldn't comprehend, in your hearts, you would know it, but you wouldn't believe it. What happened here. I was so worried about this.

There is one face you will see, if you look for her, a tall woman who looked right into the camera—we were all being moved, shoved, shot at, from the trains, children crying, old people falling to the ground and being shot, we were in shock, terrified, cowed, cringing, but this woman?

She glared. With her strong face and piercing eyes she GLARED RIGHT into the camera, her FACE was PURE intelligence, her face was saying I know who you are and I am not afraid of you. History will judge you.

And do you know, this woman is outside right now, on this day of liberation, she is... can you hear her? She is beating one of them to death with a shovel, and this time, the Allies are filming this, and she is looking at the camera, but with a different face, a face of triumph, a face of THIS IS MY... moment. And what you did to us? Will never never happen to us again.

At the time, I understood this woman. If I had been strong enough, I would have BEEN this woman.

Now, whenever I hear about the terrible things our soldiers have done, in the name of revenge.

I see her face. I see only her face.

BLANDY (calls Leopoldina) Hey, Leopoldina, I know, you're in the subway, so your phone don't work, but if you listen to this message before you get here, I wanted to say, I got this remembrance hittin' me, Leo. Remember, 'member our first communion, remember the stupid white dresses we wore? With the lace veils? An' shiny white shoes that KILLED my feet? And even the GLOVES. And how we ate that white layer cake and inside our piece of cake we each got a silver quarter? Ummm... I just remembered that and I wanted to say? Even if you don't make it tonight? You are my best best best friend in the whole world and... I love you like a planet exploding!

SORELE   While my sister was in prison, she wrote me a letter; my friend Hana, she bribed the guard to look the other way and she brought it to me. I had to tear it to pieces so they wouldn't find it.

She was afraid. She was afraid to die.

BLANDY   I hope they don't do nothing to my eyes.

They'll all have their cellphones, and they will get this on the cellphones, and then they will send it to YouTube and the whole world gonna hear the last words of Blandy. Last song of Bernadette.

They gonna see my face, bloody, and my nose broken, but they will not see me cry, they will not see me cry, and they will not ever see me beg for my life.

Never never never never never.

SORELE   *(to BLANDY)* I saw her hang, I saw the rope break her neck. I closed my eyes. I closed my eyes but they opened. I

46

heard, I heard the gypsy girls hammering, sawing, all day long from my hiding place, constructing, making the scaffold, the gallows where my sister would breathe her last breath; I was hiding on the floor under a bunk, my mouth on the dirt floor when they came into the block and ordered us out: "Raus, raus," their dogs growling; "Raus, raus." The Slovenian kapo, she pulled me out by my hair, "Dirty little Pole." I am standing among a thousand other women and girls, the January wind tearing through us, I wanted only to disintegrate into the wind, to vanish like Ariel and blow away, far away with my sister. At dusk they brought them out, the sky was violent blue-grey; Ala, Rosa, Regina, and my sister; they all seemed to shimmer, walking strong, tall, heads high, faces bright! My SISTER, when I saw her I felt her hot morning breath on my neck, the way it was when we shared the same bed at home, I smelled her hair, her sweet head. I was screaming, screaming in my mind, for help, from our father, our mother, knowing that no help would come. They brought her up first, she looked only at us; into my eyes miles deep, and as she stepped up, like lightning striking, there was a blade in her hands, gleaming in the dusk, she smiled wide and threw up her wrist and with the blade SLASHED, SLASHED at her wrist, blood spraying out, and slashed the throat of the SS, he's in shock, she speaks, her voice thundering, an archangel.

BLANDY   You can have my body but you will never never have my life; I will NEVER let you take my life.

Never never never never.

BOTH   NEVER.

BLANDY   *(assuming the voice of SORELE's sister)* "YOU will die like a COCKROACH in a matter of days when the ALLIES come; I will die with DIGNITY by my OWN hand, knowing that you have not touched my soul, you can never touch our souls!"

SORELE   And then she turned to the thousand girls and women.

BLANDY   "They can never touch your souls!"

SORELE   We were not watching their hanging, what we were watching was their souls, swirling out of their bodies and into the air around us, shimmering, moving into our own poor bodies and souls.

> *BLANDY hears something, the sound of a big band of girls, threatening, with rap music.*

What I believed, lying here in the pile of dead bodies, is that we who have suffered unthinkable cruelty will never be cruel to others.

BLANDY   If it be now, 'tis not to come;

SORELE   That we who have been hated...

BLANDY   If it be not to come, it will be now;

SORELE   ...will never hate.

BLANDY   If it be not now, yet it will come!

SORELE   And that is why,
That is why I opened my eyes.

And I raised my hand.
And now,
In… hope?
I raise my hand again.

BLANDY   Hey, can you feel the shimmering?

SORELE   "Oh brave new world!" That's what I said when the medics came.

BLANDY   Hey, Rochelle, Lisa, Annette, Divora, Leanne!

SORELE   "That has such people in it!" They looked so beautiful!

BLANDY   *(Her crowd gets louder.)* I am so glad to see you. Listen, I got somethin' wicked to tell you: it's the secret, the secret of the world.

> *BLANDY is violently punched twelve times, with each sound of the church bell. The girls run away.*

> *BLANDY collapses. SORELE goes through the fence as her fifteen-year-old self, being freed from the camp, to BLANDY, and comforts her. They help each other up, SORELE becoming her fifty-five-year-old self. They look at each other.*

We defy augury.

> *The end.*

Acknowledgements

I would like to thank Nightswimming Theatre: the brilliant and patient Brian Quirt; the woman who can make things happen, Naomi Campbell; and, of course, the awe-inspiring Michaela Washburn and Marcia Vacratsis. Thanks also to Andy McKim and to all of the folks at Passe Muraille.

author photo by David Laurence

Judith Thompson is a two-time winner of the Governor General's Literary Award for *White Biting Dog* and *The Other Side of the Dark*. In 2006 she was invested as an Officer in the Order of Canada and in 2008 she was awarded the prestigious Susan Smith Blackburn Prize for her play *Palace of the End*. Judith is a professor of drama at the University of Guelph and lives with her husband and five children in Toronto.